THE
AIRMAN'S
WORLD

Gill Robb Wilson

Random House
New York

ENDPAPER PHOTOGRAPH by Jim Yarnell

TITLE PAGE PHOTOGRAPH by Ben Kocivar

Library of Congress Catalog Card Number: 57-10030

Parts of this series originally appeared in *Flying* magazine.

Printed In The United States of America
By The Murray Printing Company

*To all who from the beginning created
and in the present sustain and
in the future fulfill human destiny
on the skyways of the universe
this book is dedicated.*

Introduction

The airman's world is founded on perspective. His viewpoint differs from that of the earthbound. To a pilot the hazard of a thunderstorm is its turbulence. To a man on the ground the hazard of the same storm is its lightning stroke. To a mariner a South Sea atoll lying in the mists of a Pacific dawn is a thing of which to beware. To a pilot the same atoll is a reassuring check point on his way to destination. To an office worker a low ceiling may mean good acoustics. To a pilot it may mean his neck. The glow of a great city approached at night may be a scene of splendor to the traveler. To the pilot it is something else as his eyes search for the running lights of other planes against the maze of winking signs below.

Likewise, the airman accumulates knowledge of the world at a rate incredible to the earthbound, who can hardly comprehend that a pilot, in the routine of his toil, may be equally well-acquainted with Bubbling Well Road of Shanghai and the Puerto del Sol of Madrid and the lovely Avenida Beira Mar of Rio de Janeiro and the Maidan of Calcutta as with Main Street. He has seen that the shape of the family hut in New Guinea is a tribal identification; that the aborigine along the headwaters of the Amazon is cursed with toothache; that the bushman of outback Australia can follow a trail by scent; that a camel caravan in North Africa is a good place to barter for ancient coins and icons; that the Chimora children of Guam are exceptionally attractive; that New Zealand meadows are a pastoral paradise; that the biggest oranges grow on Crete; that the stone huts of Eric still stand in Greenland; that the secret of the Viking ship was the iron rivet; that America was discovered by virtue not of the compass but of an infrequent wind current; that the Eskimo of King Island is a master craftsman in ivory; that there is a jade mountain in outer Alaska; that the ancient jousting ground of Richard the Lion Hearted stands intact on Cyprus near the mountain castle of Queen Berengaria.

The airman is not necessarily a fisherman but he well may have landed a ten-pound rainbow trout at Naknek, or speared shark off Samoa, or watched the whales at play in the North Atlantic, or snagged supper out of Peru's three-mile-high Lake Titicaca, or struggled to boat a fighting salmon in a Norwegian fiord.

He is not necessarily a hunter but he has ridden after the great wolf dogs on the steppes east of Ankara, and gunned for duck on the Bosporus, and circled the polar bear on the floes off Point Barrow, and, with the stick between his knees, leaned out a cockpit window to take pictures of the scampering wild life on the African veldt.

The airman perhaps never pored over ancient history but he has flown the trails of Tamerlane, and the treks of Alexander, and marked the conquests of Cyrus and Hannibal, and lowered his flaps in the land of the Pharaohs and of the Incas and by the Great Wall of China. His sole source of knowledge may be that he has been there, but the lore has rubbed off on him and is authentically his. Of such stuff is the airman's world; and I have barely hinted at its fascinations.

The scope of the airman's world is not complex. He has two very simple if revolutionary abilities at hand. One is to compact time, the other is to telescope distance. His ability to rendezvous over any point on the globe is a matter of gas in his tanks rather than of intervening obstacles—oceans, mountains or deserts. His freedom and flexibility to go and to know is something new in human activity.

On the other hand, the airman has vital considerations which are of scant concern to the earthbound. His evaluation of the natural phenomena which he encounters must be knowledgeable. He must be an *air* man in addition to being a pilot. The speed and direction of the wind have causation factors. He must understand them. The

nature and portent of cloud, the evidences of building storm, the indications which eventuate in fog are matters with which he must deal. The rotation of the globe, the effect of ocean and land masses on the atmosphere wherein he cruises are basic to his airmanship. And to all these considerations and many more he must relate the capability of the ship he pilots and his own skill in its control.

The process of becoming an airman is never completed, never satisfied. But it molds the inner man even as it affects his physical existence. One can not become a citizen of the airman's world and remain oblivious to the larger vistas which continuously reach out beyond present realization. The future will be as the airman makes it. He has the tools.

It is not then mere poetic license to speak of the airman's world—an area of perspective and experience which is still uniquely the possession of the pilot and crewman but which gradually is being penetrated by such as airline passengers, businessmen and the families of airmen.

Perhaps I should establish my own authentic right to speak of the airman's world. I have been at home in the sky for more than forty years. I flew with the French and United States forces in the first of the great modern wars and have been about the affairs of aviation in many capacities since that time—as pilot, official, war correspondent, and in scores of related administrative, advisory, educational tasks. These years have been wonderful in accumulation of the knowledge of many lands and peoples and of the sky itself. I have come to know the length and depth and breadth of my own land as few have been privileged to know it. And above all, memory is forever at flood tide with the comrades of the long years—those with whom I have fought and played around the world—men with sweaty palms and weather beaten faces and the wisdom of airmanship in the seat of their pants and fingertip skill at their command.

It goes without saying that this book of glimpses into the airman's world is their story rather than mine alone; and that it has been a boon of fortune to walk with them—the continuing generation of an endless breed that throughout human history has had to see over the hill or die trying.

Perhaps I should lower my gear at this point and land. But I think there is something more that might help the reader to understand the central motivation of the airman's world.

In its origin, flight was an object in itself. However, that period was soon eclipsed. A decade after the first airplane was flown, the nations of the world were girding for war. A comparative handful of pilots flew in that conflict but upon those who did, friend and foe alike, it was borne in that a revolutionary new force had been introduced into human affairs. The crudity of the aircraft of those days went unnoted in the all engrossing conviction that the airplane held the key to the future for better or worse. Time would take care of its perfection for whatever utilities might be desired. The pertinent fact was that the sky was a new medium of destiny, a frontier where hitherto only the mythologist and poet had dared set foot. Such a prospect excited the minds and stretched the imaginations of young airmen. Today they tell me that every student pilot may forget all else but never his first solo flight. I have not the slightest memory of my first solo and I doubt that many of my confreres of early days remember theirs. The miracle of flight was so engrossing that indoctrination was a step to be hurried over as a matter of scant consequence except as a stepping stone.

To emerge from wartime flying was of course a relief. The occupational hazards of early piloting, to say nothing of combat, required luck for survival. Why then did the young pilots of the several combatant powers, and there were no other pilots at that time, permanently leave the various professions and occupations for which they had been educated in pre-war days and follow the will-o'-the-wisp—a designation for aviation which had almost universal credence at the time?

The reason was very clear in their minds, if in the minds of no others. They were convinced that the nations which most effectively staked out their futures on the air frontier would inherit the leadership of the earth. Each nation's airmen felt a deep responsibility in this respect, for toward this end they represented their country's sole asset. Each of the several national groups returned from war to speak not of individual experiences but of the new frontier of civilization—the sky.

The German group apparently told their story best. At any rate, defeated Germany was soon expansively aloft around the world in commerce and, since science is indivisible for peace or war, in military potential. The mighty Luftwaffe was an inevitable consequence.

The young pilots of democracy found no such fertile soil. Triumphant governments felt no great urgency. Nevertheless, the airmen crusaded and won kindred spirits of the oncoming generation to their ranks. With their recruits they barnstormed and set the stage for community airports, and raced and tested and used their airplanes for discovery, and authored aviation organizations, and projected commercial enterprises, and pondered on military strategy without ceasing.

Private pilots were missionaries for commerce; military pilots originated crop dusting; airmail pilots taught students between runs; and any and every airman was a John the Baptist to proclaim the coming of the new day. Slowly but surely the airplanes improved in performance, in dependability, in utility. And progressively the airman hewed out the perspective that is the airman's world and learned to come and go with increasing safety and certainty to the ends of the earth.

I think it is well to remember that the airman's world was founded on a motivation beyond love of adventure, beyond flying for flying's own sake, beyond even the honest purpose of livelihood. That it has been a motivated world has made it none the less an area where men and women have found high exhilaration and infinite satisfaction—an area where one might find adventure in such measure as he or she sought; a world of self-examination; a world whose ultimate reaches know no bounds.

It must be a world of high compensations. I have lived in it for most of a lifetime and have envied no man who walks the face of this earth. Could one seek or find more?

The Airman's World

The Atmosphere

Essential to life upon our planet
is the broiling blanket of the atmosphere,
the all-encompassing air ocean, whose
nearer shore is the land and sea beneath,
and whose farther shore is outer space.
Redeemed from ageless mysticism
by the pressing curiosity of man, the air ocean
is become lordly to human destiny
in fact as once in fancy.
Eternally in motion, here rises the shield
against the cosmic avalanche,
here filters the sun of poison,
here brews the climate of harvest.
And here at long last
is the physical medium of one social family.
Not since time began has civilization been
so challenged in mind and spirit to exhaust
the potential of the physical universe
as in the air age. Nor is this challenge
one of easy accomplishment.
A heart for the unknown,
a courage for the unexpected,
and a will to see over the next hill—
these are essential equipment of the airman.
Yet the rewards are unparalleled . . . .
frescoes of cloud and shadow such as man never painted,
the grip of forces such as man never created,
a sense of freedom such as man never dreamed.

The Upflung Highlands

The upflung highlands
are the jewel casques of nature.
Among them in haunting secrecy
lie the souvenirs of her liveliest caprices
and most melancholy moods—
white-laced waters tumbling from one snow bank
toward separate oceans;
canyon depths without a ray of sun in a million years.
And as outer sentinels of her inner treasure,
as if to anticipate the coming of the airman,
nature has set the strong winds,
the cunning currents, the thin air and
the smoke screen of ever shifting cloud.
Yet, as if to reward the respectful
and the knowledgeable and the skillful,
nature betimes quiets the wind and draws back
the cloud and bids the thunder be still.
In such times the wise may go with safety
over the highlands, and the memories
will be commensurate with the privilege.
For as long as life may last
one will recall the crag smoothing the lines
from his brow in the mirror of the crystal lake;
or the high peak rearranging the feathers
of his snow plume after the storm, or the great forest
cracking his knuckles in the deep cold.
And because these and a thousand more frescoes
remain indelible on his mind, the airman
has his own jewel casque of inner resources.

Bill Susoeff, North American Aviation

The Prairie

The prairie is the diaphragm of the land
and upon its swelling breast the nation
was nurtured to empire. Here the red man was
cradled in the bounty of the Great Spirit
and departing bequeathed his shining names to mark
the divisions of our tenantry—
Michigan, Wisconsin and Wyoming,
Illinois and Iowa, Oklahoma and Dakota,
Kansas, Nebraska and myriad others.
Came in time the covered Conestogas
and the groaning Pittsburghers,
the cattle trails and winding rails
and paddle wheels churning the rivers;
came too the plows and fences
and ribbons of yellow road. And the buffalo grass
gave way to the endless sweep of grain.
So today the sights and signs
and divisions of habitation are so multiple
that scant concept of the prairie
as the warrior and plainsman knew it
can be got by the traveler on the surface.
But not so with the airman
swinging high over the prairie land.
To him the detail of habitation is merged
in the mists of distance and he may see
how the prairie folds interminably wave after wave
to the far curvature of the spinning earth.
Yet on him also the prairie places a tax.
Here sweeps the strongest wind in unobstructed flow;
here towers the highest thunderhead;
here breeds the fiercest turbulence.
The killer tornado hides behind the soft breeze
and the yellow dust storm obscures the land and sky.
Thus the airman who sees the prairie
as the Sioux and the pioneer saw it.
must know alike with them, its moods and caprices.
In such knowledge is written
the textbook of the airman's lore.

H. Armstrong Roberts

The River

*"We will give the names of our fearless race
To each bright river whose course we trace..."*

So sang Felicia Hemans in her Song of Emigration,
and although the unhappy English girl of long ago
never saw America and its rivers,
she truly sang of us—of Susquehanna and Suwannee,
of Columbia and Colorado, of Missouri
and Mississippi, of Red and Rogue and Rio Grande,
of Tombigbee and Trinity, of Platte and Powder
and Wichita and Wabash and a thousand more.
And to whom but the airman is it given to see
how the silver threads winding far beneath his wing
shaped the primeval patterns of travel,
divided the boundaries of sovereignty,
decided the issues of war
and apportioned the powers of nature.

How happy is our vista—
to mark their distant courses by the canyon wall,
or trace them over the prairie
by the green hemstitch of cottonwood and willow
or note in the piedmont the mist of their breath
at sunset or in the dawn.
And if at times the river confuses us
by turning back upon himself
or hides his course beneath a veil of fog,
he more often orients us on the path to destination.
But, regardless, the airman must count the river
among his tutors of heart and mind
in things beyond the skill of the cockpit.

For is it not true, you airmen of this land,
that we who are privileged to watch it
in continuous panorama, bisected river by river,
must come inevitably to brood over it?
In what eternal origins
rise the currents of our destiny
and to what eternal source do they return
in the fullness of time? Shall this land fade
as all before have faded
in the fragmented patriotism of their peoples?
Or may we, custodians of fresh perspective,
better trace in our time
those currents of truth and freedom
which are the silver threads
of enduring empire winding down the years?

For let it be known that of such verities,
as well as of more material things,
is the airman's world composed.

The Wind

The wind, ah the wind,
the fretting of that ocean upon which
the high mariner is embarked. And though
this restless architect of dune and desert,
this scourer of mountains and sweeper of seas
is obedient to primordial law,
it is its vagaries rather than its exactitudes
that make the wind the most exciting force in nature.
The aerologist names the wind
by the points of the compass; traces its origins
to the pattern of atmospheric density
around the earth; and tells us how
the tilting of the globe upon its axis seasonally
displaces its zonal field of activity.
But you and I are not philosophers of global wind.
We are its children,
more affected by its caprices than its origins.
We meet it at runway's end, over the high hills,
down in the valleys and burbling on the shore lines.
It is there that it tests and teaches and teases
until we no longer overcontrol for gusts,
no longer fly straight over the ridges,
no longer drive up the center of valleys.
So, if the wind is a polisher of peaks,
it is also a polisher of pilots.
If it is a stylist of nature,
it is no less a stylist of navigators.
If it disciplines the marching dunes, how much more
it calls the cadence to our goings and comings.
In mythology, Aeolus was nominated
the controller of the winds.
Eos, Goddess of the Dawn, was their mother,
and their father was the Titan, Astraeus.
But you and I know how vain are prayers to Aeolus,
or to Eos or the Titan.
Not to control the wind, but to control ourselves
as we are challenged by the wind
in skill and judgment and alertness,
is the test of our stature in the airman's world.
And if we roam far afield to meet the Sirocco,
the Chinook and Pampero, the Mistral and Föhn
   and Bora,
we only confirm our belief that
the airman's world has no compare short of
the last great venture to the shores of eternity.

Patterns

Patterns, patterns, patterns—
you've seen a million of them—
highway patterns, power-line patterns, reforestation
patterns, patterns of contour plowing,
strip-mine patterns, oil-field patterns—
and on the way over to Salt Lake this morning
you saw a pattern you had never before noticed,
a design of tiny gray holes in the high waste country,
like a punchboard on a dirty restaurant counter.
That was a pattern of uranium mining.

You reflect that you first began
to understand the world when, abroad in the war,
you became conscious of the patterns—
the island patterns, the jungle patterns,
the rain patterns, the patterns of sea and sand,
of graze and grain, of arctic and tropic—
the patterns that make men and nations
what they are or aspire to be.
So you came to see why peoples are backward
    or forward,
fierce or friendly, dependent or independent.
The patterns had voices for one
who saw them in high perspective
and now they are symbolic of your outlook on life,
pages in the book of your experience.
It would be futile to tell the earthbound
that you would dry up inside if you couldn't fly—
if you lost contact with the patterns.
None but old pilots could understand
that you live in a habit of perspective.
How could anyone else reckon what it's worth
to know the patterns—
the patterns of rivers deflecting to create deserts,
the patterns of valleys retreating to form harbors,
the pattern of wind flowing to form climate,
the pattern of marshland creeping
to the will of the tide—
and the big pattern of all things
melding and molding and singing and sobbing
to make man and his universe what they are.
No, you can't expect the stripling to evaluate
that kind of gold, or wingless men
to mark that the gray in your thatch is really
the silver you minted from the patterns.
A man must have some inner satisfaction
whose god is not the measure of the world.

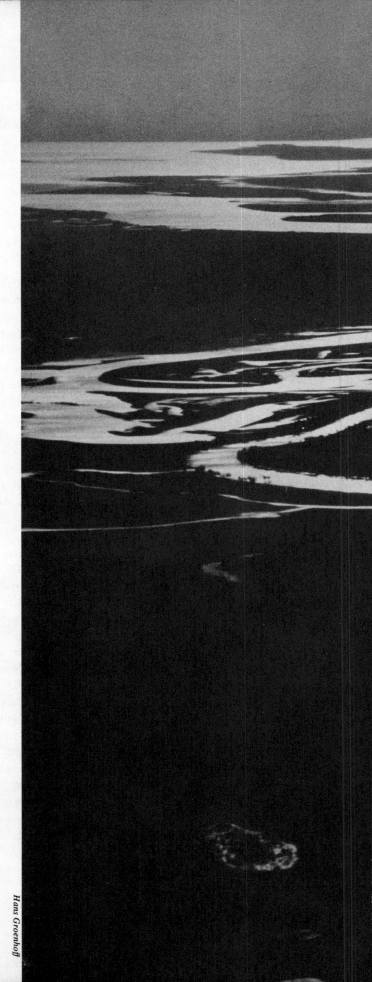

The Everglades

Where the mood of the tropics
reaches up a warm wet finger toward
Yanqui land, lies the great labyrinthine
marsh, the Everglades—four thousand
square miles of brooding mystery,
multiform in sawgrass plain and islands
of wax myrtle, willow and live oak;
and in a mosaic of bright waters
to publish the mortgage of the sea
which once slept here, as indeed you may
see for yourself swinging at ten thousand
feet from Okeechobee to the Gulf.

And when you have flown so many
years that your engine no longer goes on
automatic rough each time you are beyond
glide to some airport, you may wing
above the great swamp and lend your heart
and mind to ecstasy of blending colors
and intricate patterns.

Abandoned by the mother sea
and never claimed by the father land,
the orphaned marshes, lonesome through
the eons, nurture their paleolithic
heritage with a haunting pathos
that, once meditated upon from far aloft,
you will understand.

And when you have understood,
the grunt of the alligator will be to you
a farewell to yesterday
and the bawl of the calf at the edge
of the cane field a brave hail
to tomorrow. But all in good time only,
for the marsh is in no hurry,
catholic alike to sea and land.

Wayside Trees

Wayside trees in a rain-lashed night
Twigged for the winter's snow,
Sleeping the sleep of the interstice
Till the winds of April blow . . .

But the view is not a wayside scene.
It is the tributaries of a great river
as the airman sees them from aloft.
Above and beyond
all intriguing fancies and resemblances
is the fact that much becomes intelligible
when the mind embraces far vistas
and marks the significance of their detail
in its effect upon the story of man.

Coursing above some departed empire,
one may see why it grew overconfident
and thus decadent; or one may see what element
of relative permanence it never had.
The logic of genius or fallacy in the deliberations
of those who walked before us and made
their decisions from an earthbound viewpoint

is an open page. Flight for the sake of flight
leads on from physical adventure
to intellectual opportunity and one begins to apply
the advantage of great vista to his own times—
and often trembles. I judge that the habit
of far perspective as developed by one or another
people of our era will determine the course
of the future for centuries to come.

To make pilots of airplanes is not enough
for the security of the great verities
and the abiding truths—or even for the peace
of mankind. To make pilots of civilization
is the function of flight.
The cockpit is the cradle of the future
and who rocks there now
will inherit the horizons of tomorrow.

Robert Simons

The Man's the Thing

The storm—the peaks—the stratus out ahead—
the high Sierra winds—and you.
Yet one may go with such occasioned tumult on the way,
if first he's won the victory o'er himself.
Therein the touchstone of the airman's world.
I've been aloft since flight was young
with bamboo strut and warping wing and singing wire.
I've seen the hills bow down,
the seas constrict, the rivers rage,
the winds become the whimpering slaves of trade.
I've peered in nature's restless heart—
the jungle dank, the coral reef,
the mountain gargling melted rock,
the meteor dust on ageless ice,
the flaming torch of Arctic night,
the myriad suns of northern day.
I've seen the lightning born, the iceberg whelped,
the sky turned purple as it starved for air.
But this I've never seen—
a mountain high as my unreasoned fright
when lack of judgment trapped me unaware;
a jungle dank as my foul self-contempt
when panic took my mind;
a sea as broad as that remembered guilt
when careless gesture fouled my mission's plan;
a coral reef so lonely as my heart
when I had tossed away a victor's chance.
No den of dangers is this sky of ours,
demanding dark ordeal of mind and soul;
but neither trollop for the weak and vain,
the boastful proud, the arrant fool.
There is no valid license for the churl.
No unearned rating saves the palsied hand.
No title, grade or rank bestows a boon.
The man's the thing!
If he be right, the sky cannot be wrong.

The Shrine

A million years of rolling time
conspired to build an ageless shrine
upon a desert plain.
They hewed it from a mountain's heart
with patient care and skillful art
but gave it neither road nor gate
for pagan feet to desecrate.

By day they set the furnaced sun
to forge away the mountain's shale,
while night employed his frosty breath
to form and fashion rich detail,
with wind to polish each façade
to mirror Him whose shrine they made.

Still lost in solitude it stands
impervious to human plans
and so shall stand for aye,
while I who come with vaunted power
to spurn its crest have but my hour
and then, despite this winged dower
shall pass—for e'er away.

The Volcano

Prior to the air age,
as earthbound man gazed skyward
from his traditional inability to escape it,
the volcano was an avenging cloud by day
and a consuming pillar of fire by night,
with connotations of an angry God
prematurely loosing atavistic fires
in impatient sentence of the sinful.

As the airman gazes earthward from aloft,
where he may approach the red chimney
with inquiring and dispassionate mind—
and indeed this is the gift of the wing
in many matters beyond the works of nature—
he sees not the hot breath of a mad deity
but the relief of such vast pressures
within the convulsing bowels of the earth
as might otherwise blow the whole to ash.

It is the stamp of the airman's coin
that he is lifted to gain understanding
and to shed the fearfulness of ignorance
accrued from the foreshortened vision of yesteryear,
when there was no measuring rod of dimension,
to see all things in large relationship
—the days when men cajoled a moody God
and fawned on the inanimate forces
and fled because they dared not draw near.

The Sunkissed Valley

You've been cruising the brooding hills
under heavy skies—
maybe a little lonely and a bit uncertain—
when suddenly the westering sun
finds a rent in the canopy overhead.

Long after you've forgotten
the sweat of the journey, you'll remember
the glimpse of that sunkissed valley
with the fingers of the hills all pointing to it.

When you've flown enough years to have
crossed many hills and valleys, and known much
loneliness and endured many uncertainties—
why then you're a pilot.
You can never be too much afraid of what lies ahead.

Just as the fact of flight telescopes time and space,
so the experience of flying telescopes
the pattern of life itself for the airman.

If you don't venture on sullen skies,
you never come to sunkissed valleys.
If your palms have never been moist,
your heart has never thrilled.

If you have never been afraid,
you have never been courageous.

You have seen primordial forces at work
beyond the control of any man,
but you have fashioned a skill
to live with them in security and peace.
You have sensed that where there is no challenge
there is no achievement.

So I think he learns of life,
this one with the seven-league boots,
this airman who goes from place to place

with such swiftness that even the moods of the sky
are caught up in his going and coming.

And if it does not mold him
in humility of mind and in peace of heart—
and if he does not become in spirit
at one with the fingered hills
pointing eternally to some bright human hope
which nestles in the shadows of a sullen history—
then I have not read with understanding
the long, long thoughts of my confreres—
they who have earned
a citizenship in the airman's world.

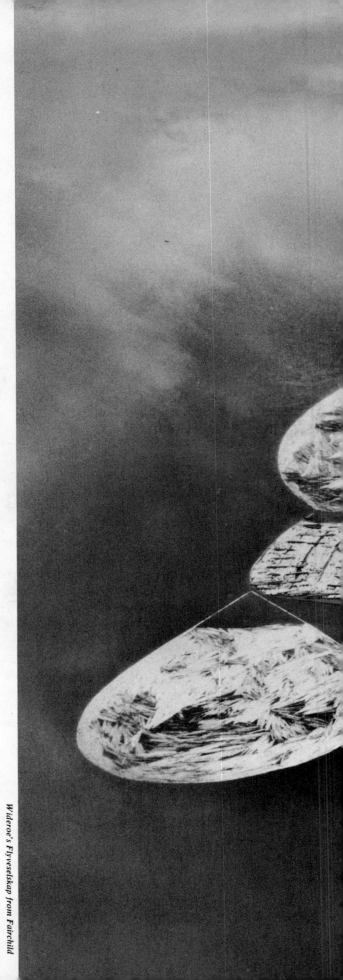

The Army of Trees

An army of trees from the crested hills
march down the waves to the hungry mills,
battalioned in cunning array to stride
with the cadence called by the wind and tide,
and sensitive as a gay ballet
to the maestro's wand, as they curve and sway
to the will of the helmsman, who leads the way.

And to this my wing gives audience,
and the primitive grace is recompense;
and who in the world but such as we,
who roam the skies with a fancy free
ever may see such artistry.

A mountain gives to a desert plain,
in a distant place, his heart in spring,
and I trace his subterranean hand
reached out to his love beneath the land
with a bright bouquet for the yellow sand;
and I muse that this I share alone
with those who watch from the judgment throne.

And to this my wing gives audience,
and a pilot has his recompense,
for who in the world but such as we,
may climb the sky to God's own knee
and ponder his wondrous artistry.

The airman deals in geography.
Geography is the mother of the old cities.
Immemorially earthbound, men have linked their lives
where land and sea have blended most happily;
where deep rivers have made confluence;
or at crossings of strategic trails.

During many centuries the great cities
exercised authority over civilization—
social, political, economic, spiritual.
And in the first half-century of flight,
the airplane bowed to the pattern of Piccadilly
and Times Square and the Piazza Venezia
and the Puerto del Sol and the Bund.
To make one street of the Avenue des Champs-Elysées
and Michigan Avenue and Avenida Beira Mar
seemed enough. And it was enough
so long as the airman's trail led along
the nearer shore of the air ocean,
where the winds and storms and fogs of the
    lower atmosphere
beat like surf against the globe.

But it is no longer enough.
The airplane is launching now
on the farthest reaches of the air ocean
above the vagaries of the atmosphere.

More and more it overflies even the mightiest cities
to follow great circle courses
to global destinations.

The need is gone to circumvent broad seas
and desert wastes and arctic ice.
The old cities have lost their unshakable authority
over the destiny of man.
They totter in stature before the logic of the air age.
In vain they spend their substance
in the loved features of their obsolescence.
In vain they relegate the facilities
of the air age to their outermost limits.

In the rolling years their accustomed stature
will recede. The air age will build new cities
nearer to its heart's desire.
The old city is a target, not of the atom bomb,
but of the airman's geography.
Some day in the far future, a pilot,
noting the position of his aircraft in space,
will say to his passengers over the microphone,
"Beneath us at this point
lies one of the seven wonders of the earthbound age,
the ruins of New York.
The city was never under military attack,
and many features are well preserved."

The Pursuit of Happiness

Hither and yon above our landscape
searching out the sweetness of life,
like bees over a meadow of white clover,
wing more little planes than take the air
in the combined remainder of the world,
theirs a pursuit germane to the whole unfolding
human story—the pursuit of happiness.
It is neither adequate nor accurate
to suppose that those in the little planes
are flying for the sheer fun of it.
Of a certainty they find moments of lightness
of heart since the pursuit of happiness

is rarely a grim ordeal, but their satisfactions
touch a deeper chord than gaiety alone.
I can feel a pity for him who has never looked down
upon the sweep of it all until he lost
consciousness of its divisions by deeds and titles
and townships and counties and murmured to himself—
this is my land, my home land, my country.
I can have a sadness for him who has never
lost himself in the deep glory of
"thy rocks and rills, thy woods and templed hills."
I can feel cheated for him who has no awareness
of the land as it changes its garments in season

and washes its face at the spigoted clouds,
and nurtures its myriad forms of life.
Once upon a time the man in the Ercoupe
was a boy in a Liberator over Schweinfurt
or in a P-47 over Iwo Jima.
He was about the business of buying a future
for himself—and for the land now beneath his wings.
That was indeed grim business.
But this is what he bought
and it is anything but grim—
this Maryland countryside of his on a summer's day—
this corner of his airman's world.

The Ancient Sentinel

To the man in the cockpit the scene
is ever changing and beckoning for attention,
sometimes from the sky
and sometimes from the land or sea.

High on a peak above the canyon
where the ribbon of river boils among the boulders,
the ancient tree keeps sentinel,
leaning far out from the rock as if to peer
at his own roots laced viselike
in the crevice which cradled him.
A thunderhead is dissolving below him
and out on the opposite ridge
the cumulus is preparing to tower for another.
I should clear out of here
but the old tree will be something to remember
when this flight is long forgotten.

I will remember how he stands
in the fretting sky and disdains to die.
I will remember that the tall must expect the pain
they avoid who grow on the sheltered plain.
I will remember that they have gales to face
who choose to stand in the highest place
and that the proud must scorn that scars accrue
to heads held high where lightnings brew.
I will remember that be it man or tree,
the good life is lived where one can see
deep and far
to the canyon's heart or the midnight star.
I will remember that the storms may come and go
but that I shall grow
while my roots are fast in the sod:
to the tree, in the mountain—to me, in God.

Heritage

Of the lore that accrues to the airman
with his seven-league boots, none is more soul-
filling than the inexhaustible romance
of the men and women who built this America.

It is no slight thing to live
conscious that one is born to the purple—
that one's heritage is a record of proud courage
in the face of adversity, and of vision
which saw through impenetrable forests
and past high-flung peaks. In older lands
this pride is escutcheoned by title and crest
but for me here only in a single flag of stars and stripes.
And it is my own true lineage;
none the less so for its blending of creeds and breeds.

I might have learned of Mountain Men
and of the Voyageurs—of Carson and Clark
and Whitman and Bridger and Freeman
and Pike and a hundred more, from dusty pages.
I might have gained from ancient maps
some knowledge of how ran the trails—
the Appalachian, the Santa Fe, the Oregon,
the Chisholm, the Tennessee Trace and
a score in addition. But flight has made them mine
in their contours and contexts, in their demands
and in their rewards. I have been able to hear
tossing herds of longhorns wending to railhead
across Oklahoma; the shout of the bullwhacks
on the banks of the Snake and the crack
of the 15-shot Henrys
in the thickets along the Big Horn.
I have been made to understand the conflicts
of men and of governments for a continent.
I know whence a declaration which looked
to the ideals of a united humanity from the background
of a mere un-united thirteen colonies.

The wing is a pedagogue whose texts
are endless and whose illustrations live and breathe,
uncircumscribed in time, to him who will go and read
whence his heritage and whither its fulfillment.
But if he goes not, or in going sees naught,
then let him adjure the wing.
It is not for them who are content with pottage.

To Be Free

The fun of it! Oh, the fun of it!
The soul-cleansing, mind-clearing fun of it!

To climb in the cloud-flecked sky
and roll off to scream down
into the black bowl of night
until the red line nudges you to ease gently out
and reach for altitude again.
And there, over your upswung nose,
the man in the moon beckoning you to keep coming
but smiling benignly because he knows
you will never make it.

You have freedom enough
without climbing to the moon—as yet.
You have broken away from the spider web below.
The river is naught but a silver thread
caught in the needle eye of a moonbeam.
The winking lights of earth
are as the flitting of fireflies
in the meadows of your youth.
You are free, free, free!

But the best is yet to come.
Way up there you swing in wide circles
under the stars.
It is better than rest, than sleep—
this solitude, this ecstatic aloneness.

The cares and frettings drop away
into the consuming eddies of the lower air.
You are in the cathedral where the ear perchance
    may hear
the music of the spheres
coming downwind from eternity.

Some say it is the resonance of your propeller
and some say it is the imagination of a pilot,
but I say it is the break-through of a heart
at peace with the mysteries beyond.
I have held my breath in suspended wonder
lest I miss, for a flash of seconds
the swelling chorus of praise
to Him from whom all blessings flow.
I have even thought at times
that I could distinguish the clear tenor
or the deep bass of some historic voice
that had been foremost among men on earth
to proclaim the great verities—
faith and courage
and the fraternity of all things.

And if this seems strange to you
who have never looked at the moon through a
    climbing propeller
or heard the music of the spheres—
come see and hear and doubt no more.

Portrait
of Private Pilots

Lo, a portrait of private pilots—
they who love the sky for its own sake—
mark of the true airman.
Overhead an Arizona thunderstorm
builds to dark conclusion.
To go or not to go—that is the question.
But the life of a private pilot
is full of questions!
On a thousand reaches of sky
I have seen them through the years,
bucking over the high ridges,
weaving down the canyons, washboarding the prairies,
landing on the glaciers.
They quaff the lore of far places in hungry gulps,
fill their souls with length and depth
and breadth of the land,
and test themselves with the variations of it.
Among them, if nowhere else in the air age,
romance is the great reality.
At every opportunity they consort together
as if holding a common secret—
as indeed they do.
But if you sought to define their bond,
you would not find the words.
Not even they could tell you. Nor can I.
But this I can tell you.
Theirs is a bond of the spirit,
an eagerness shared, a partnership of restlessness
to know challenge and motion.
Some men go down to the sea in ships
and find tranquillity of mind.
And some sit on a high hill
or tramp autumn fields for the good of their souls.
And what these find in land and sea,
the private pilot finds in the ever changing
frieze of the overhead, in the nudge of the wind,
in the vista from "on top"—
and in the freedom to go.
Long may their breed increase.

The Sailplane

Where the lace of the waters is stitched to the land
by the throb of the tide in the sea,
and the earth in erosion lends scallops of sand
to ruffle the surf that is hemmed to the land—
the fingering zephyrs will be.

And here in the atmosphere's ambient change
and the local effect of the continent's range,
the sailors who sail on the ocean of air
with naught but their knowledge to carry them clear—
assemble their sensitive planes.

What is formed in the instinct of gull and of tern
by the cunning of nature, the sailor must learn,
and the art is less matter of knowledge to fly
than of being at home with the moods of the sky—
and patience to learn.

Here, absent the surge and the roar of the screw
and advice from the tower and the help of a crew;
here only the lisp of the wave on the sand
and the whisper of zephyr upswept from the land—
and your art and you.

Don Downie

The Happy Lonely

If a young man were to ask me of the qualities
essential to an eager and happy career as an airman,
I would pass quickly from physical condition
and aptitude to dwell at length
upon an intangible quality for which
I have no name other than character fitness.
A part of this character fitness
would have to be a capacity for happy loneliness,
a capacity unrued by most. Yet when I pause
to name the gifts bestowed by years aloft—
to tell my rosary of things that linger on—
I must in truth give thanks for this.
For what is poignant in the things
that one remembers—Paris, Rome, Singapore—
the Taj Mahal, the Pyramids, the Parthenon—
the majesty of the Rockies, the sullen heights
of the Urals, the black waters of the Tasman,
the glory of the setting sun on Great Barrier Reef?
Ah no, my lad, not these, not these—
not the man-made things nor the majesties of nature.
What then is poignant above all?
Why, the lonely lighthouse on the far northern cape
where you circled once to bring the wave of a hand
as your gift to a fellow spirit.
Why, the outrigger canoe tossing far from land
on the swells of the South Pacific
and the Polynesian who raised his paddle to you
in the kinship of lonely people.
Why, the Eskimo on the ice floe north of Nome
and his crouching dogs—and you wondered
if you had been unkind perhaps
in spoiling his stalk of a seal at the blowhole.
Why, the handful of crew on some lugger
bucking a North Atlantic blow—
or a fishing dory out of Reykjavik—
or some forest ranger whose lookout tower you circled
in the high country. It is such as these,
the happy lonely, who are with you
when the wingtips are buried in white nothingness
and the ice is building and the static has taken over.
If you have heart for them—the happy lonely—
then, lad, come to the airman's world. It is your world.

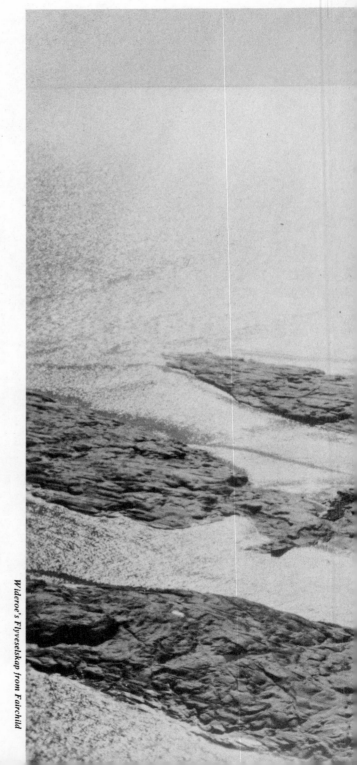

Widerøe's Flyveselskap from Fairchild

The Wind Sock

The wind was the magnet which drew
the sons of the bishop to the dunes of Kitty Hawk.
Propulsive power for their wings was hard to come by.
They drafted the wind.

But the wings were frail, and where too little wind was useless,
too much was disastrous. The first airmen had to contrive
a measuring rod of the wind—some device they could interpret
from aloft as well as from the ground.

The wind sock was the answer.
Whether Orville and Wilbur, or some other, first fashioned it
is lost lore, but it swiftly became the universal
identification of landfall for the airman.
For two thirds of the first half-century of powered flight,
the wind sock welcomed and warned the brash men and their planes.
Without exception, the ships of those years
were underpowered and the airman played the wind
as he no longer does. He came over the field lower
than low to read the message of the sock,
pulled up into a chandelle, chopped his power, slipped steeply
to the ground and kicked his nose into the wind
as he sat down in a full stall.
It was fun to do, lovely to watch and saved shock cord
and wire wheels from taxiing on rutted fields.

The wind sock is passing now—
gone with the goggles and the starting booster and the tail skid
and the biplane itself—gone with the gunnery roll
and the falling leaf and the Jenny Immelmann—
gone from almost everywhere except the nostalgic memory
of the breed which had no runways and no tricycle
gear and no tower to identify them as a blip on a scope
or give them a number in a stack or reassure them
on glidepath, as they groped with dusty tanks for a glimpse
of the ground and a flicker of motion that was a wind sock.

But this is progress and it is good.
The wind sock was often a creation of caprice.
In turbulent air it would wrap itself around the pole
and dare you to guess the gusts. In icing conditions it would
freeze fast with sleet and tell you lies.
And in too much wind it would shred away
to bits of whipping rag. But it was what we had.

Owen Billman

The Gallant Clan

The futile wings on the yellowed prints
seem foolishly quaint and crude
unless one walked in the bygone years
with the sky's strange brotherhood
when there was no script or reasoned code,
when there was no center stage
where a man had a way to make his day
stand tall for another age.

They pored and peered in their patient rote
as the dreamer is wont to do
and borrowed a buck if they had the luck
to find you with more than two.
They burned the oil in the midnight lamp
but scarce earned daily bread
and often died when they tried to ride
their designs in the overhead.

So smile if you will at the weird machine
but not at the gallant clan
which gave its heart though it lacked the art
and the tools for a better plan.
They reached for the stars while the savants slept,
and their faith was a thing of flame
which kindled the sky, though today they lie
unmarked by the world's acclaim.

The Text of the Wing

My memory's of a hundred ships.
I hear the song of the wind in the wire
and the drumming roll of the gear on the meadow sod.
I smell the pungent exhaust of the castor oil
and the banana fragrance of the patch
on the punctured wing. I reach out and warm my cold hand
in the blue flame from the exhaust that leads back
from the cowl. I wipe my goggles of the rusty water
that boils from a laboring engine.
And I refresh my heart as does he who drinks again
from the spring of his boyhood.

For these were my teachers,
and they had a text beyond the skill of the flying.
They taught of the virtue
of patience with frailty, and of tenacity in decision,
and of coolness in danger.
Seven times seven they forgave my sins
and compelled me to humility.

I have heard these ancient ones
called crates and kites and cages—
but not by those they taught.
They nurtured me a thousand hours
before I ever saw a chute.
Does that bespeak a qualm?
If they were slow, they still were
swiftest of all things on earth.
And if they labored on the sky,
how else might one be lifted up ten thousand feet
above the highest hill?
If they were frail, what other petard ever
hoisted youth from where he saw far down the years
the certain vision of a changing world?

The warp wing Caudron was a caprice in the gust,
the Nieuport shed his linen in a dive,
the Jenny asked a favor in a stall,
the Waco liked to flatten in a spin.
The Mail Wing had a narrow-treaded gear.
But if each took some special pilot skill,
yet each taught something more than skill alone.
And in the ultimate they built
a happy band that loved life most—
too much to hoard it for some distant day
when years have rusted all of us away.

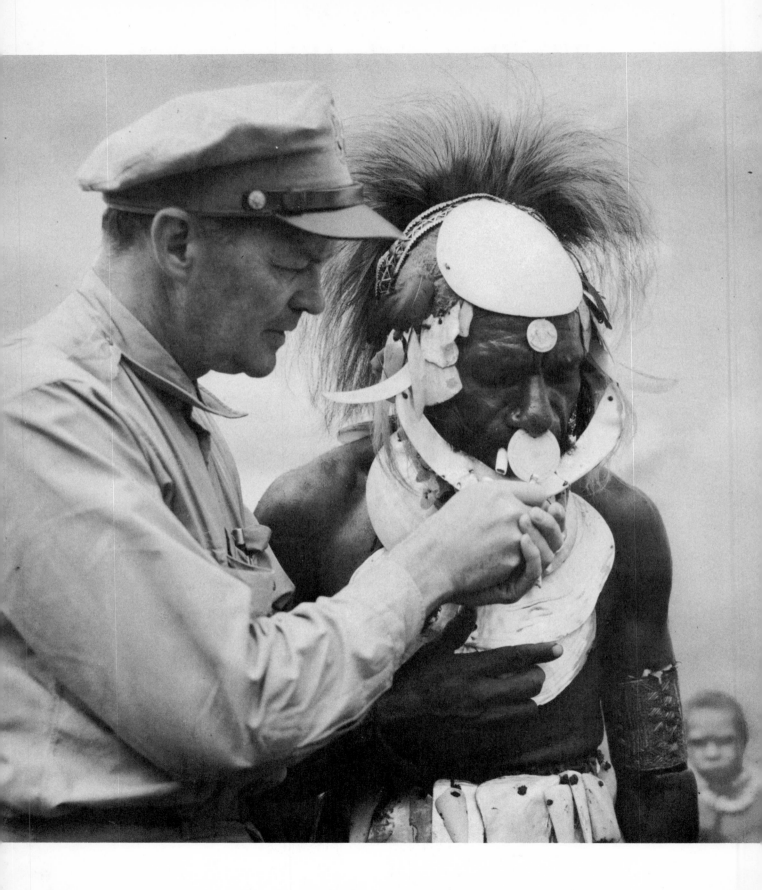

Beyond Beyond

Where the roads retreat
from the hoary peaks
and the trails fade out
in the fetid swamp
and the prow turns back
from the latticed shore,
the wing goes on and on.

And if you've heart for the things that lie
out there in the lap of time,
and if you'd see what the outer gods
have wrought beyond beyond,
and if you deem there's more to know
and much to be understood—
then take your wing and come with me
to the fringe of the brotherhood.

Out in the chartless Guinea hills
the pigment is in reverse;
black is the mark of the royal line
and clothing a useless curse;
and the drums give tone to their hopes and fears
as you lower your wing where the jungle clears
to meet the naked men with spears
who come to the native bourse.

You have no creed or code or law
to share with the Stone Age clan;
and all you know is that they, like you,
are made in the mold of man;
so you arm your face with a friendly smile
and you open your hand to deny your guile,
and the ages shrink for a little while
out there beyond beyond.

Ben Kocivar

One of the Trusted

You are at cruising altitude.
The westering sun is pink on the disk.
Your eye flicks the gauges. The engines are contented.
Another day—another dollar.

You look down at your hands on the wheel.
They are veined and hard and brown.
Tonight you notice they look a little old.
And, by George, they are old. But how can this be?
Only yesterday you were in flying school.
Time is a thief. You have been robbed.
And what have you to show for it?
A pilot—twenty years a pilot—a senior pilot.
But what of it—just a pilot.
Then the voice of the stewardess
breaks in on your reverie. The trip is running full—
eighty-four passengers—can she begin
to serve dinner to the passengers?

The passengers—oh yes, the passengers.
You noticed the line of them coming aboard—
the businessmen, the young mothers
with the children in tow, the old couple,
the two priests, the four dogfaces.

A thousand times you have watched them
file aboard and a thousand times disembark.
They always seem a little gayer after the landing
than before the take-off. Beyond doubt
they are always somewhat apprehensive aloft.
But why do they continuously come up here
in the dark sky despite their apprehension?
You have often wondered about that.
You look down at your hands again
and suddenly it comes to you.

They come because they trust you—
you the pilot. They turn over their lives
and their loved ones and their hopes and dreams
to you for safekeeping.
To be a pilot means to be one of the trusted.
They pray in the storm
that you are skillful and strong and wise.
To be a pilot is to hold life in your hands—
to be worthy of faith.

No, you have not been robbed.
You aren't "just a pilot." There is no such thing
as "just a pilot." Your job is a trust.
The years have been a trust.
You have been one of the trusted.
Who could be more?

The Airman's Campus

The airman's campus is ten miles tall
and the ivy twining its vaulted wall
has root in the breath of the misty strand
and the filtering fingers of land.

Its bounds are a scimitared edge of blue
which the eye may forge from a distant view,
and its walks are traced by the contrail's frost
till the footsteps pass and the track is lost.

Its windows look to the compassed space
where the orbiting worlds are held in place
and made to glow by the beams that run
a trillion miles from the burning sun.

Its field of play is the purple plain
where the ear may catch the sphere's refrain
to the verses sung by the dancing stars—
and the thundering bass of Mars.

The savant day and the long-haired night
hold class for the campus neophyte
with a text fresh writ each dusk and dawn
from the primal code they draw upon.

So come ye here who have heart to tread
in a tall man's pride with the thunderhead
and walk the scimitared edge of space
till the yearn of your heart finds peace.

Carrier Pilot

No, gentle reader, the airplane did not
fly through a tunnel nor is the figure with arms
suppliant to heaven calling upon Providence
to witness how truly dead center
the pilot hit the hole. This is the downwind end
of a flat-top and the worshipful figure
is a traffic cop signaling the harried jockey
to fold his wings and get the hell out of the road
before his playmate to the rear is waved off
and the landing signal officer
given an excuse to chew out the plane handler.

It is not enough that certain of our brotherhood
face the vagaries of wind and cloud. Some there are
who insist on navigation without check points
and landing on heaving airports of scant dimension.
These are called carrier pilots and, in addition
to breaking them free from the care
and feeding of offspring for long periods
at a time, their choice of doing it the hard way
makes them among the best pilots in the world.
If they get lost, they bury themselves
at sea and maintain a fine old tradition.

Ben Kocivar, Look

The discerning may distinguish a carrier pilot
from others of his ilk by the fact that all noses
are broken at the bridge and all teeth
forward of the molars are spare parts.
This is due to the time-honored custom of missing
the arresting gear and running into the barrier.
Overshooting civilian and Air Force pilots may
share this fate but, because of cockpit variances,
do not conform to patterns of physiognomy.

Upon occasions when I have been seduced into
riding with these fellow critters whose goings and
comings are sudden and abrupt, I practice
a comforting formula. The basis of this formula
is to commit my soul to God, my better judgment
to the dogs, and my body to a tight shoulder harness.
With these matters arranged in sequence of importance,
I am then free to ponder on such trivia as
the distance and direction to the nearest shore,
the survival limits of the water temperature beneath
and the comparative voracity of shark and barracuda.

Briefing

Ahoy there, you who write the books
and ponder on definitions of airpower!

I'll brief you on airpower
straight from the horse's mouth. Still squinting
from the sun on top, still stiff from
the dog fighting, still grimed from the cockpit,
still marked with the headings—
I'll tell you about airpower.

Airpower is the models you built as a kid,
the dreams you nurtured as a boy,
the freedom you craved to go out and beyond.

Airpower is the chatter in the ready room
before the horn blares, "Pilots! Man your planes!"

Airpower is a faith
that your flight leader won't pile you in on target.

Airpower is the split-second pressing
of a button to get home a deflection shot.

Airpower is the comfort of your earphones,
the fit of your chute,
the dependability of your wrist watch,
the steady fluctuation of your oxygen dial.

Airpower is confidence in the plane you fly,
confidence in the "old man" who sent you on the mission,
confidence in yourself.

Airpower is the skill and devotion
of a crew chief, the respect of your squadron mates,
the lift of love in the letters from home.

Airpower is a million little things
which merge like molecules of molten metal to form a spar
for the wings of your spirit.

But there is something more to add,
the final thing that tempers all the rest.
You must believe that, bigger than yourself,
enduring when you're gone, surviving though you perish,
your cause is right and just.

There is no power on earth or sea or sky
that can be power such as the airman needs
without convictions. The integration of his faith
with all his skill of trade—
well, such is power aloft.

God in your guts, good men at your back,
wings that stay on—and Tally Ho.

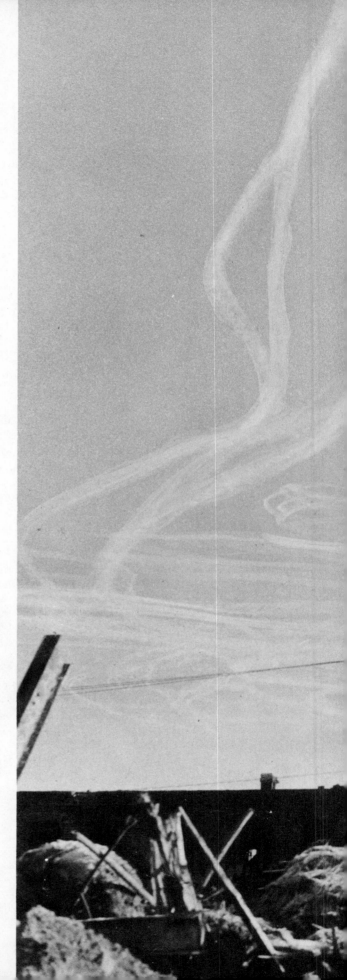

Air Force Photo

Rendezvous Over Aldenhoven

If you were skirmishing ahead of the bombers
one winter morning of the great war
and met the interceptors of the Luftwaffe
over Aldenhoven, Germany—
this is the blueprint of your toil and theirs.

Surging to the ears of the troopers below
came the scream of your engines rising in crescendo
under the torture of combat throttle
or sinking to a rhythmic whisper
as you retarded throttle in the buffeting of the dive—
and the savage exclamation of the guns
as the twisting and rolling and spinning
of the embattled brought one combatant
into the sights of another.

Swiftly the high wild passion was spent
as it raged from thirty thousand feet
to the level of the sugar-beet fields.
And suddenly the blue vault
would become quiet and untenanted
except for a score of dark threads
trailing down to the horizon—
spoor of the valiant dead—
the plunging pyre alike of friend and foe.

But even as the watching soldiers
turned again to their earthbound chores,
came the swelling drone of the bomber waves
to wash against the battlements of Festung Europa,
and their millions of harnessed horses
trampled out the last faint traces
of your rendezvous with eternity
over Aldenhoven that winter morning.

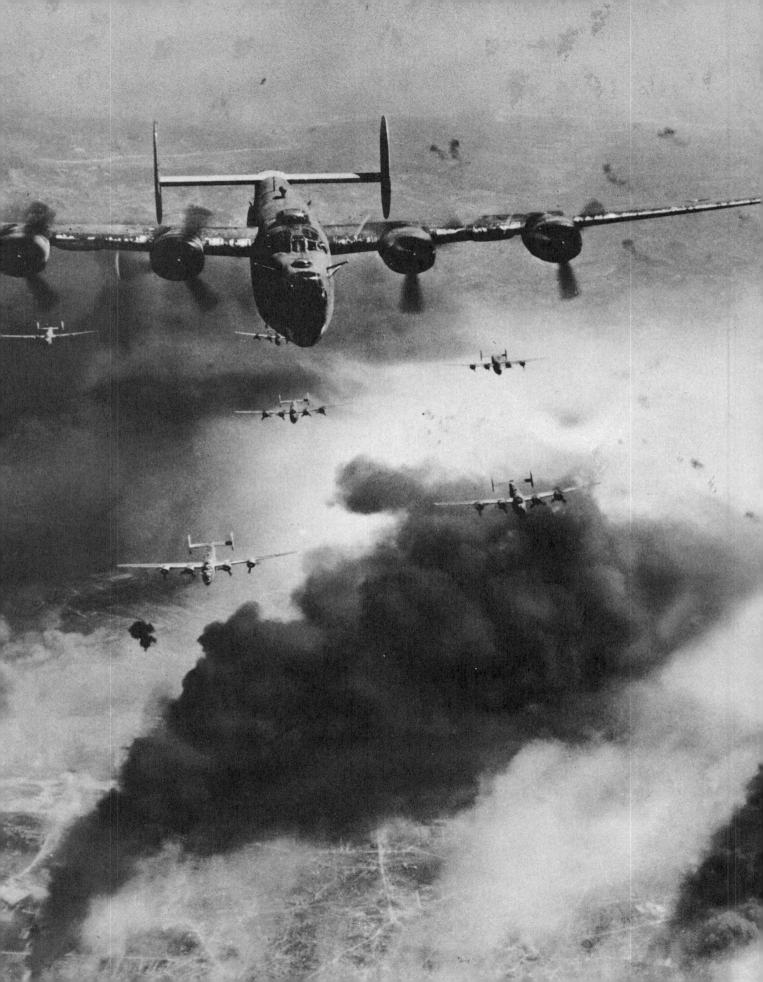

Courage

God loves the brave. At my mother's knee
I learned it from the Book of Remembrance. To serve
"with all thy heart and all thy mind and all
thy soul," one must go into the high places to hear
voices; one must search lands of new promise;
one must face the unknown with confident heart;
one must battle giants and one must be ready
to die in the very dawn of a brighter day.

Our fathers had read the book!
"Oh, say, can you see, by the dawn's early light . . ."
they sang with freedom at their backs
as they set compass west to possess a cradle
for the dreams of their children.

And now we, the children,
in turn set our feet upon the quest;
and we are challenged as none before.
The illimitable sky winnows our souls. The high
places are higher. The far places are farther.
The unknown is more mysterious.
The giants are more cunning.
And although the new day is radiant,
the watchword is still courage—
courage to seek, courage to endure
and always courage to die.

The poets and minstrels are at a loss
to sing our sagas. There have been no high casements
from which to follow our questing;
no battlements from which to mark our strivings.
The airman forges the fates in a vast loneliness.
The horizons swallow him.
His spoor is a flick of light in the sun
or a murmur of overtone in the wind.
And when the people send us forth to war,
there drifts down from the misty sky somewhere
the flotsam and jetsam
that hints of the living or the dead,
the victor or the vanquished—
and that is all. God, who loves the brave,
is alone with the brave.

To Find Myself

When the time comes that you look
back down the trail in nostalgic wonder,
remembering the accumulated hours and
the far places and the almost forgotten ships
you have flown—when you recall the
judgments and decisions, some right and some
fearfully wrong—when you relive the
accented moments of exhilaration
and breathcatching awe or the mingled ones
of hope and despair—when word for word
there comes to mind accompanied by
the dull chatter of long-silent guns
some muttered snatch of prayer—
then you must ask yourself as have I—
what did I seek that I had to find in the sky?

What did I have to know that made me
lift with hammering heart and uncertain skill
against the thermal tides—what beyond
the written page was there to learn besides—
whom did I hope to meet and make my friend
in the vast solitudes of space—
what was there to be had that I must claim
from the distant market place—
and, if the sights and sounds and smells of all
the earth around remained beyond my ken
and wondrous names conjured no memories to my
mind, what were the odds—
was life not pleasant on the land and sea
that I should seek the sky—
what did I have to find that I should fly?

Not that I have a pride in what I found
or that some find less in nearer scenes and
more familiar plans—but for me
the skies were the promised lands and I had
to know how a heart must hush to hear
the voice from the burning bush—
and I had to know what the mountain said when
a humble man bowed down his head—
and I had to go where the giants dwelt to see
how a man with a slingshot felt—
and I had to lift my timid soul to learn
if the clod comprised the whole—
and now I know what I sought to find that
made me walk with the sun and wind—
it was myself, myself.

About the Author

Not long after the Wright brothers successfully propelled their flying machine above the ground, Gill Robb Wilson made his first solo flight. With it began his unique career dedicated to aviation.

A pilot with the French Escadrille 66, he became a flying officer in the U. S. Second Army Bombardment Group after United States entry into World War I. He covered World War II for the *New York Herald Tribune* as war correspondent and aviation columnist.

Mr. Wilson was chairman of the first Aeronautics Committee of the American Legion, director for fifteen years of the New Jersey Department of Aviation, and as consultant to the Government on lighter-than-air development, made the first national airport survey. He was four times president of the National Aeronautic Association, co-founder and director of the Aircraft Owners and Pilots Association, and president of the National Association of State Aviation Officials. He created the plan for the Civil Air Patrol and organized it nationally.

President of the United States Air Force Association, Mr. Wilson is also consultant to the Training Command of the USAF, and for twenty years has been a consultant to the Air Force and Department of Commerce. He was a member of the Congressional Aviation Policy Board and is now serving as vice-president of the Air Force Historical Foundation. For many years he has been editor and publisher of *Flying* magazine.